C1a Topic 1 — The Earth's Sea and Atmosphere

Pages 1-2 — The Evolution of the Atmosphere

Q1 True statements: When the Earth was formed, its surface was molten.
When some plants died and were buried under layers of sediment, the carbon they had removed from the atmosphere became locked up in carbonate rocks.

Q2 The percentage of carbon dioxide has decreased by a large amount because it dissolved into the oceans and green plants used it for photosynthesis.

Q3 The statements should be in this order (from the top of the timeline):
1. The atmosphere is about four-fifths nitrogen and one-fifth oxygen.
2. The build-up of oxygen in the atmosphere allows more complex organisms to evolve and flourish. The oxygen also creates the ozone layer.
3. Green plants evolve over most of the Earth. They're quite happy in the CO_2 atmosphere. A lot of the CO_2 dissolves into the oceans. The green plants also absorb some of the CO_2 and produce O_2 by photosynthesis.
4. Water vapour condenses to form oceans.
5. The Earth cools down slightly. A thin crust forms. There's lots of volcanic activity.
6. The Earth's surface is molten — it's so hot that any atmosphere just 'boils away' into space.

Q4 a) Largest sector is Nitrogen, second largest is Oxygen, smallest is Carbon dioxide and other gases.

b) Nitrogen: 80% approx (to be more precise, it's 78% in dry air)
Oxygen: 20% approx (to be more precise, it's 21% in dry air)

c) Nitrogen has increased. Carbon dioxide has decreased. Far less water vapour now. Oxygen is now a significant proportion of the atmosphere.

d) As the planet cooled, the water vapour condensed and formed the oceans.

e) Plants and microorganisms photosynthesised and produced it.

f) In any order:
Created the ozone layer which blocked harmful rays from the Sun.
Killed off early organisms/allowed more complex ones to evolve.

Page 3 — Today's Atmosphere

Q1 a) i) One of: burning fossil fuels / deforestation

ii) One of:
Burning fossil fuels releases carbon dioxide into the atmosphere, causing the level to rise. /
Deforestation means there are fewer trees removing carbon dioxide by photosynthesis.

b) Generally increased, although it has fluctuated.

c) No-one was around millions of years ago so we are making guesses based upon evidence like bubbles of air trapped in ice.

Q2 About 40 cm³. Air is 20% oxygen so about 10 cm³ would be used in the reaction (20% of 50), leaving 40 cm³.

C1a Topic 2 — Materials from the Earth

Pages 4-5 — The Three Different Types of Rock

Q1 igneous rocks — formed when magma cools — granite
metamorphic rocks — formed under intense heat and pressure — marble
sedimentary rocks — formed from layers of sediment — limestone

Q2 Crust, slowly, big, intrusive, quickly, small, extrusive

Q3 a) E.g. the church is made from limestone which is formed mostly from sea shells.

b) The pressure forces out the water. Fluids flowing through the pores deposit minerals that cement the sediment together.

c) They are both made from the same chemical.

Q4 a) 1. Possible uplift to the surface
2. Pressure from rocks above
3. Metamorphic rocks forming here
4. Intense heat from below

b) Metamorphic rock has a hard, even texture.

Q5 a) True

b) False. They are formed over millions of years.

c) False. Chalk is a sedimentary rock.

d) False. Igneous rocks are harder.

e) True

Q6 Limestone and chalk are sedimentary rocks which aren't formed at high temperatures, so the fossils aren't destroyed by heat.

Pages 6-8 — Using Limestone

Q1 glass, cement and concrete

Q2 a) Any two from: noise, dust, loss of habitats for plants and animals, increased traffic and noise / pollution from lorries.

b) Quarries provide employment for local people which can provide a boost to the local economy. There may also be improvements to infrastructure such as roads, recreational and health facilities.

Q3 a) neutralisation

b) The limestone removes sulfur dioxide from the smoke emitted from the power stations. This helps to reduce acid rain.

Q4 a) The limestone in the Peak District is very pure.

b) About 1.6 million tonnes (7.9 ÷ 5 = 1.58).

c) It is used in agriculture and burned in lime kilns.

d) i) canals and railways

ii) by road / by lorry

e) Answer will depend on student's opinion, but they are likely to say that they are against it because the article focuses on the problems associated with quarrying rather than the benefits it has.

f)

Use	Percentage	Total amount quarried in tonnes
Aggregate (for road-building etc.)	52%	(7900000 ÷ 100) ×52 = 4108000
Cement	24%	(7900000 ÷ 100) ×24 = 1896000
Iron and steel making	2%	(7900000 ÷ 100) ×2 = 158000
Chemicals and other uses	22%	(7900000 ÷ 100) ×22 = 1738000

C1a Topic 2 — Materials from the Earth

Pages 9-10 — Limestone and Thermal Decomposition

Q1 a) Thermal decomposition is when one substance chemically changes into at least two new substances when it's heated.

b) Calcium oxide will react with water to give an alkaline substance. You could prove this using universal indicator (it would turn blue or purple). Calcium carbonate would remain neutral.

c) Pass the gas produced through limewater. The limewater will go cloudy/milk/white, proving that carbon dioxide is present.

Q2 a) calcium carbonate

b) calcium oxide, carbon dioxide

c) zinc oxide

d) copper carbonate → copper oxide + carbon dioxide

Q3 a) calcium carbonate → calcium oxide + carbon dioxide

b) To neutralise soils that are acidic.

Q4 a) 1. Heat the carbonate in a boiling tube.
2. Pipe off the gas into a test tube of limewater.
3. Record the time taken for the limewater to change colour.
4. Repeat for each carbonate.
5. Compare your results.

b)

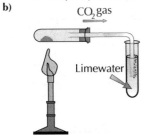

CO$_2$ gas

Limewater

c) i) The limewater would turn milky more quickly for the carbonate that decomposed the fastest.

ii) Some carbonates are more stable than others. Less stable carbonates decompose more readily.

d) A colour change, as some carbonates are a different colour to their oxides.

Page 11 — Atoms and Mass in Chemical Reactions

Q1 atoms, particles, atoms, rearranged, mass, constant.

Q2 a) A precipitate is an insoluble solid that forms in a solution.

b) copper sulfate + sodium hydroxide → copper hydroxide + sodium sulfate

c) **27 g** (12 g + 15 g)

Q3 a) **11 g** (29 g – 18 g)

b) yes

Pages 12-13 — Balancing Equations

Q1 a) Correctly balanced

b) Incorrectly balanced

c) Incorrectly balanced

d) Correctly balanced

e) Correctly balanced

Q2 The third equation should be circled.

Q3 a) The reactants are methane and oxygen, and the products are carbon dioxide and water.

b) methane + oxygen → carbon dioxide + water

c) $CH_4 + 2O_2 \rightarrow CO_2 + 2H_2O$

Q4 a) $2Na + Cl_2 \rightarrow 2NaCl$

b) $4Li + O_2 \rightarrow 2Li_2O$

c) $MgCO_3 + 2HCl \rightarrow MgCl_2 + H_2O + CO_2$

d) $2Li + 2H_2O \rightarrow 2LiOH + H_2$

Q5 a) $CuO + 2HBr \rightarrow CuBr_2 + H_2O$

b) $H_2 + Br_2 \rightarrow 2HBr$

c) $2Mg + O_2 \rightarrow 2MgO$

d) $2NaOH + H_2SO_4 \rightarrow Na_2SO_4 + 2H_2O$

Q6 a) $3NaOH + AlBr_3 \rightarrow 3NaBr + Al(OH)_3$

b) $2FeCl_2 + Cl_2 \rightarrow 2FeCl_3$

c) $N_2 + 3H_2 \rightarrow 2NH_3$

d) $4Fe + 3O_2 \rightarrow 2Fe_2O_3$

e) $4NH_3 + 5O_2 \rightarrow 4NO + 6H_2O$

Pages 14-16 — Mixed Questions — C1a Topics 1 & 2

Q1 a) i)

ii) $CaCO_3 \rightarrow CaO + CO_2$

iii) In the laboratory as a test for carbon dioxide.

b)

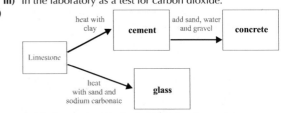

c) Acid rain reacts with the limestone and causes it to dissolve.

d) i) Limestone is turned into marble when very high temperatures break it down over a long period of time. The limestone reforms as small crystals.

ii) 1. Marble has a more even texture and is harder than limestone.
2. Unlike limestone, marble doesn't usually contain fossils. The high temperature it is formed at destroys them.

Q2 a) No. There was virtually no oxygen so today's complex organisms couldn't survive.

b) green plants

c) increasing, carbon dioxide, burning, reduces, absorbed.

d) i) False, only 1% of the atmosphere is noble gases.

ii) True

iii) False, plants take in carbon dioxide and give out oxygen during photosynthesis.

e) No-one was around millions of years ago so we can only make guesses and theories.

Q3 a) s

b) l

c) g

d) aq

Q4 a) $ZnCO_3 \rightarrow ZnO + CO_2$

b) $2Cu + O_2 \rightarrow 2CuO$

c) $CaO + H_2O \rightarrow Ca(OH)_2$

Q5 a) Place the reactants in a flask sealed with a bung. React copper sulfate with sodium hydroxide to produce a precipitate of copper hydroxide in sodium sulfate. Weigh at the start and end of the reaction. Compare the two measurements — there should be no change in mass.

b) Thermal decomposition of carbonates produces carbon dioxide gas. If the apparatus was not sealed this product would escape, and so it would seem as though the reaction mass had changed.

c) No atoms are lost or gained. They are just rearranged.

C1b Topic 3 — Acids

C1b Topic 3 — Acids

Page 17 — Hazard Symbols

Q1 a) false
b) true
c) false
d) true
e) false
f) false
g) true

Q2 a) — corrosive — attacks and destroys living tissue.

b) — irritant — causes reddening or blistering of the skin.

c) — toxic — can cause death if swallowed, inhaled or absorbed through the skin.

d) — oxidising — provides oxygen which allows other materials to burn more fiercely.

e) — harmful — like toxic but not quite as dangerous.

f) — highly flammable — catches fire easily.

Page 18 — Acids and Alkalis

Q1 a) acidic
b) acid
c) base
d) water
e) 7
Q2 a) purple — 14 — strong alkali
b) yellow — 5/6 — weak acid
c) dark green/blue — 8/9 — weak alkali
d) red — 1 — strong acid
e) green — 7 — neutral
Q3 a) Baking soda or soap powder, because they are weak bases and so would neutralise the acid but wouldn't irritate or harm the skin. Stronger bases like caustic soda might damage the skin.
b) E.g. the colour can be difficult to judge exactly.

Page 19 — Hydrochloric Acid and Indigestion Tablets

Q1 Missing words are: digestion, acidic, kill, too much, base, neutralise.
Q2 a) B — 15.9, C — 23.4, D —16.7, E — 6.6
b) Tablet E
c) Tablet E
d) Tablet C is most effective because a single dose neutralises the largest volume of acid.

Pages 20-23 — Reactions of Acids

Q1 acid + metal hydroxide $\rightarrow$ salt + water
Q2 acid + metal oxide $\rightarrow$ salt + water
Q3 a) hydrochloric acid + lead oxide $\rightarrow$ **lead** chloride + water
b) nitric acid + copper hydroxide $\rightarrow$ copper **nitrate** + water
c) sulfuric acid + zinc oxide $\rightarrow$ zinc sulfate + **water**
d) hydrochloric acid + **nickel** oxide $\rightarrow$ nickel **chloride** + **water**
e) **nitric** acid + copper oxide $\rightarrow$ **copper** nitrate + **water**

f) sulfuric acid + **sodium** hydroxide $\rightarrow$ sodium **sulfate** + **water**
g) hydrochloric acid + **calcium** hydroxide $\rightarrow$ calcium **chloride** + **water**
Q4 a) $CuO_{(s)}$
b) $H_2O_{(l)}$
c) $HCl_{(aq)}$
d) $ZnO_{(s)}$
e) $Na_2SO_{4(aq)} + 2H_2O_{(l)}$
f) $KNO_{3\ (aq)} + H_2O_{(l)}$
g) $H_2SO_{4\ (aq)},\ H_2O$
Q5 a) $H_3PO_4 + 3NaOH \rightarrow Na_3PO_4 + 3H_2O$
b) $2NaOH + H_2SO_4 \rightarrow Na_2SO_4 + 2H_2O$
c) $Mg(OH)_2 + 2HNO_3 \rightarrow Mg(NO_3)_2 + 2H_2O$
d) $2NH_3 + H_2SO_4 \rightarrow (NH_4)_2SO_4$
Q6 acid + metal carbonate $\rightarrow$ salt + water + carbon dioxide
Q7 a) nitric acid + sodium carbonate $\rightarrow$ **sodium nitrate** + **carbon dioxide** + **water**
b) calcium carbonate + hydrochloric acid $\rightarrow$ **calcium chloride** + **carbon dioxide** + **water**
c) **zinc carbonate** + sulfuric acid $\rightarrow$ zinc sulfate + **carbon dioxide** + **water**
d) nitric acid + **magnesium carbonate** $\rightarrow$ magnesium nitrate + **carbon dioxide** + **water**
e) copper carbonate + **hydrochloric acid** $\rightarrow$ copper chloride + **carbon dioxide** + **water**
f) **magnesium carbonate** + **sulfuric acid** $\rightarrow$ magnesium sulfate + **carbon dioxide** + **water**
Q8 a) chloride
b) nitrate
c) sulfate
Q9 a) $CuCO_{3(s)}$
b) $MgCO_{3(s)},\ CO_{2(g)}$
c) $ZnCO_{3(s)}$
d) $Na_2SO_{4(aq)} + H_2O_{(l)} + CO_{2(g)}$
Q10 a) $2HCl + CaCO_3 \rightarrow CaCl_2 + H_2O + CO_2$
b) $2HCl + K_2CO_3 \rightarrow 2KCl + H_2O + CO_2$
c) $2HNO_3 + ZnCO_3 \rightarrow Zn(NO_3)_2 + H_2O + CO_2$
d) $Na_2CO_3 + 2HCl \rightarrow 2NaCl + H_2O + CO_2$

Pages 24-25 — Electrolysis

Q1 Missing words are: electrical energy, direct current, electrolyte, electrodes, gas.
Q2 a) Hydrogen and chlorine
b) Hydrogen gives a 'squeaky pop' when it comes into contact with a burning splint.
Chlorine bleaches damp litmus paper.
Q3 a) Chlorine gas was produced in the experiment, and it is also used to kill bacteria in swimming pools.
b) Chlorine gas is toxic.
c) The experiment should be carried out in a fume cupboard / The lab should be checked to make sure it is well ventilated.
Q4 a) chlorine
b) $100 - (11 + 20 + 6 + 5 + 33) = 25\%$
c) plastics
Q5 a) hydrogen and oxygen
b) He would test the gases to show that they're oxygen and hydrogen, and that there's no chlorine present.
The hydrogen will make a 'squeaky pop' with a lighted splint. Oxygen will relight a glowing splint. Oxygen isn't produced by the electrolysis of hydrochloric acid.
He could also do the chlorine test on the gases. If neither bleaches damp litmus paper then chlorine isn't present.
These tests would prove that he wasn't using hydrochloric acid.

C1b Topic 4 — Obtaining and Using Metals

C1b Topic 4 — Obtaining and Using Metals

Page 26 — Metal Ores

Q1 a) True
b) True
c) False
d) True
Q2 Carbon (in the wood) is more reactive than copper, so it 'steals' oxygen from the copper ore.
Q3 Carbon, below, reduction, electrolysis, more
Q4 a) It is unreactive so doesn't tend to form compounds with other elements.
b) i) $3Fe + 2O_2 \rightarrow Fe_3O_4$
ii) oxidised
c) i) $2CuO + C \rightarrow 2Cu + CO_2$
ii) reduced

Pages 27-28 — Reduction of Metal Ores

Q1 a) Iron is lower in the reactivity series than carbon so carbon will displace iron from its oxide.
b) iron(III) oxide + carbon → iron + carbon dioxide
c) $2Fe_2O_3 + 3C \rightarrow 4Fe + 3CO_2$
d) Potassium, Magnesium, Calcium, Aluminium and Sodium should be ticked.
Q2 a) Name: sphalerite/zinc sulfide, chemical formula: ZnS
b) zinc sulfide + oxygen → zinc oxide + sulfur dioxide
c) $2ZnO + C \rightarrow 2Zn + CO_2$
Q3 Electrolysis — The breakdown of a substance using electricity.
Electrolyte — The liquid that is used in electrolysis.
Electrode — Used to apply electricity to the liquid.
Q4 a) True
b) True
c) False
d) False
e) False
Q5 A — d.c. source
B — electrode
C — molten aluminium oxide
D — molten aluminium

Pages 29-30 — Properties of Metals

Q1 a) Metal 3 (because it has the best heat conduction, and is strong and resistant to corrosion).
b) Metal 2 (because it is the strongest, isn't too expensive and won't corrode too much). (Accept metal 3.)
c) Metal 1 (because it is most resistant to corrosion so it will last a long time).
Q2 Desirable qualities in a metal used to make knives and forks would be: e.g. strong, resistant to corrosion, visually attractive / shiny, non-toxic.
Q3 a) low density
b) conducts heat
c) resists corrosion
d) ductile
Q4 a) A and B
b) A, because it took least time for the end that wasn't near the heat source to heat up.
Q5 Any three from: good conductor of electricity, good conductor of heat, strong, easily bendable.
Q6 Missing words are: some, oxidised, more, easily, less

Pages 31-32 — Making Metals More Useful

Q1 a) A mixture of two or more metals or a mixture of a metal and a non-metal.
b) By adding small amounts of carbon and sometimes other metals to the iron.
Q2 low-carbon steel — 0.1% carbon — car bodies
high-carbon steel — 1.5% carbon — blades for tools
stainless steel — chromium — cutlery
Q3 a) nickel, titanium
b) zinc, copper or nickel
c) gold
Q4 a) 37.5% (9 ÷ 24 x 100 = 37.5)
b) 9-carat gold is harder than pure gold because it is an alloy and so it contains different sized atoms. The atoms in 9-carat gold can't slide over each other as easily as the ones in pure gold can.
Q5 a) Fineness means the number of parts of pure gold per thousand.
b) 900 fineness is the same as — 90% pure gold.
042 fineness is the same as — 1 carat gold.
375 fineness is the same as — 9 carat gold.
750 fineness is the same as — a gold alloy with 25% other metals.
Q6 a) Any sensible answer, e.g. for making spectacle frames.
b) i) They have a shape memory property.
ii) They have an ability to return to their original shape if they have been bent out of shape.

Page 33 — Recycling

Q1 E.g. any three from: Recycling means using less finite resources.
Recycling uses a fraction of the energy that mining, extracting and purifying the original metal would.
Using less energy means recycling can also be cheaper than making more of the original material.
Recycling means less rubbish has to be put into landfill, which takes up space and pollutes the surroundings.
Q2 a) True
b) True
c) False
Q3 a) i) 4 × 1 = **4 tonnes**.
ii) 3 billion × 20 = **60 billion g of aluminium**
60 billion ÷ 1000 = **60 million kg of aluminium**
60 million ÷ 1000 = **60 000 tonnes of aluminium**
iii) about 60 000 × 4 = **240 000 tonnes of bauxite**
b) i) Mining the bauxite causes deforestation, as the mines are often located in rainforests in addition to the general pollution and damage to the landscape associated with mining.
ii) Large amounts of electricity are needed to extract the aluminium, which means a lot of fossil fuel has to be burned. This generates a lot of CO_2, adding to the greenhouse effect.
iii) This means more bauxite has to be mined and the aluminium extracted, destroying more rainforest and producing more CO_2. The waste cans would also increase the amount of landfill.

C1b Topic 5 — Fuels

C1b Topic 5 — Fuels

Pages 34-35 — Fractional Distillation of Crude Oil

Q1 a) Crude oil is a **mixture** of different molecules.
b) Crude oil contains **hydrocarbon** molecules.
c) The molecules in crude oil **aren't** chemically bonded to each other.
d) Physical methods **can** be used to separate out the molecules in crude oil.
Q2 hydrogen and carbon
Q3

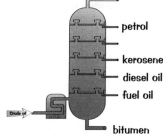

- petrol
- kerosene
- diesel oil
- fuel oil
- bitumen

Q4 The larger the molecule the higher the boiling/condensing point.
Q5 Gas: Used for cooking and heating
Petrol: Used as a fuel for cars
Kerosene: Used as an aircraft fuel
Diesel Oil: Used as a fuel for lorries, trains and some cars
Fuel Oil: Used as a fuel for ships and some power stations
Bitumen: Used to surface roads and roofs
Q6 lower, carbon/hydrogen, hydrogen/carbon, ignite, viscous
Q7 Crude oil is a finite resource and will one day run out. This means that petrol will run out too.

Page 36 — Burning Fuels

Q1 a) hydrocarbon + oxygen → carbon dioxide + water
b) oxidised, gives out
Q2 Any three from: E.g. how easily it burns / its energy value / how much ash or smoke it produces / how easy it is to store or transport.
Q3 a) CO_2 and H_2O
b) If there is not enough oxygen.
Q4 a) hydrocarbon + oxygen → **carbon + carbon monoxide + carbon dioxide + water**
b) Carbon monoxide is produced which is a very toxic (poisonous) gas.

Page 37 — Environmental Problems

Q1 Hydrocarbon fuels like petrol and diesel often contain impurities of sulfur. When they are burnt, sulfur dioxide gas is released into the air.
Q2 The main cause of acid rain is sulfur dioxide.
Acid rain kills trees and acidifies lakes.
Limestone buildings and statues are affected by acid rain.
In clouds sulfur dioxide reacts with water to make sulfuric acid.
Q3 Any three from:
E.g. removing the sulfur from the fuel before it is burnt (using low-sulfur fuels).
Fitting cars with catalytic converters.
Using scrubbers in power station chimneys to remove sulfur dioxide from emissions.
Reducing the usage of fossil fuels.
Q4 Answer will depend on student's opinion — may argue that everyone who lives on Earth and uses its resources has a responsibility to try and prevent environmental damage. Alternatively, may suggest that new technologies will be able to prevent damage.

Pages 38-39 — More Environmental Problems

Q1 True statements:
Greenhouse gases include carbon dioxide and methane.
Increasing amounts of greenhouse gases are causing global warming.
Q2 a) Global temperature has generally increased, although it has fluctuated.
b) E.g. burning fossil fuels and deforestation
c) E.g. the graph shows data collected over a long time to show that the temperature change is not just a temporary fluctuation.
Q3 fossil, an increase, CO_2, greenhouse
Q4 a) C
b) i) Cars burn fossil fuels and give out CO_2 in their exhaust gases.
ii) The TV uses up electricity so the power station has to burn more fuel, which produces CO_2.
Q5 a) False
b) True
c) False
Q6 a) seeding, injecting, phytoplankton, photosynthesis, hydrocarbons, high
b) Any one from:
E.g. there is no way of controlling what plankton grows — some is toxic.
When the plankton dies it is decomposed by microorganisms that use up oxygen, creating 'dead zones' in the ocean.
If carbon dioxide isn't converted into hydrocarbons using 'green' energy then this process just increases CO_2 levels.

Pages 40-41 — Biofuels

Q1 Biofuels are alternatives to fossil fuels. They're made from chemicals obtained from living things, e.g. living organisms' waste or dead plants.
Q2 a)

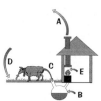

b) The plants used to produce biogas can be replaced with new plants, and the animal waste will constantly be replaced by the animals or by new animals.
c) Biogas is a cheap fuel because the raw materials (plant waste or manure) are cheap and readily available.
Q3 a) True
b) True
c) False
d) False
e) False
Q4 a) water and carbon dioxide
b) The crops needed for its production absorb CO_2 from the atmosphere in photosynthesis while growing.
c) The weather in Britain is not as good and there is not as much available land for crop growth as there is in Brazil.
Q5 a) Advantages could include:
renewable, fewer particulates emitted, don't cause acid rain, don't add as much CO_2 to the atmosphere, raw materials are cheap/readily available.
b) Disadvantages could include:
can be unreliable (e.g. sugar crop for ethanol may fail), can require large amounts of land to grow the plants / keep the animals, CO_2 is still emitted when the fuels are burned, distilling the ethanol uses a lot of energy.

C1b Topic 5 — Fuels

Page 42 — Fuel Cells

Q1 a) Oxygen: Relights a glowing splint
Hydrogen: Makes a squeaky pop when burnt
b) water
Q2 fuel, oxygen, electricity
Q3 Advantages could include:
They're more efficient than batteries and power stations.
There are no moving parts unlike in a car engine or power station so energy isn't lost through friction.
The only by-products are water and heat so there are no pollutants produced. Unlike batteries they don't run down or need recharging. Unlike batteries they aren't polluting to dispose of.
Disadvantages could include:
Hydrogen is a gas so it takes up loads more space to store than liquid fuels like petrol. It's difficult to store safely.
The hydrogen fuel is often made either from hydrocarbons (from fossil fuels), or by electrolysis of water which uses electricity (usually generated using fossil fuels).

Page 43 — Measuring the Energy Content of Fuels

Q1 a)

Fuel	Initial Mass (g)	Final Mass (g)	Mass of Fuel Burnt (g)
A	98	92	6
B	102	89	13

b) i) fuel A
ii) It takes less fuel to heat the water by the same amount.
c) i)

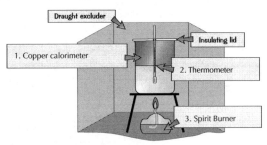

Draught excluder
Insulating lid
1. Copper calorimeter
2. Thermometer
3. Spirit Burner

ii) To reduce heat loss.
d) E.g.
1. The apparatus
2. The amount of water
3. The start and finish temperatures of the water

Page 44 — Alkanes and Alkenes

Q1 a) ethene
b)

$$\begin{array}{c} \;\;H\;\;H \\ \;\;|\;\;\;\;| \\ H-C-C-H \\ \;\;|\;\;\;\;| \\ \;\;H\;\;H \end{array}$$

c) methane
Q2 a) False
b) True
c) False
d) True
e) True
Q3 bromine water, decolourise, bromine water, brown, colourless

Page 45 — Cracking Hydrocarbons

Q1 shorter, petrol, diesel, long, high, catalyst, molecules, cracking, alkenes
Q2 a) On the mineral wool.
b) The porcelain acts as a catalyst.
c) Small alkanes and alkenes.
Q3 $C_{10}H_{22} \rightarrow C_8H_{18} + C_2H_4$

Pages 46-47 — Using Alkenes to Make Polymers

Q1 a) ethene
b)

$$n\begin{pmatrix} CH_3\;H \\ |\;\;\;\;| \\ C=C \\ |\;\;\;\;| \\ H\;\;H \end{pmatrix} \rightarrow \begin{pmatrix} CH_3\;H \\ |\;\;\;\;| \\ C-C \\ |\;\;\;\;| \\ H\;\;H \end{pmatrix}_n$$

Q2 a)

$$\begin{array}{c} H Cl \\ \backslash / \\ C=C \\ / \backslash \\ H H \end{array}$$

b)

$$n\begin{pmatrix} H Cl \\ \backslash \;/ \\ C=C \\ / \;\backslash \\ H H \end{pmatrix} \rightarrow \begin{pmatrix} H\;\;Cl \\ |\;\;\;\;| \\ C-C \\ |\;\;\;\;| \\ H\;\;H \end{pmatrix}_n$$

Q3 Poly(ethene) — Plastic bags
Poly(propene) — Carpets, thermal underwear and plastic containers
PVC — Clothing, electric cables and pipes
PTFE — Non-stick coating for pans
Q4 Cracking is the breakdown of large molecules into smaller ones, whereas polymerisation is small molecules joining to form bigger molecules.
Cracking makes small alkenes and alkanes, polymerisation often uses alkenes to make alkanes.
Cracking usually involves breaking single bonds between carbon atoms. In polymerisation, the double bonds in carbon atoms are broken.
Q5 a) Waste remains in landfill. Landfill sites are getting full and more are needed, which takes up useful land.
b) They produce toxic gases when burnt.
c) E.g. recycling is expensive.
There are lots of types of plastic and they need to be separated out before recycling.
d) The polymer could break down into products that are harmful.

Pages 48-50 — Mixed Questions — C1b Topics 3, 4 & 5

Q1 a) The following should be ticked:
Metals are generally strong but also bendy.
Metals corrode when they are oxidised.
Properties of a metal can be altered by mixing it with another metal to form an alloy.
b) i) E.g. copper is below hydrogen in the reactivity series, and so it doesn't react with water.
ii) E.g. gold is used for jewellery because it is shiny / gold is used in electric circuits/tooth fillings because it is unreactive.
c) R. The material needs to be as light and as strong as possible with a high melting point and a reasonable price. S has a low melting point. T is expensive and fairly dense. U is not very strong and has a high density.

C2a Topic 1 — Atomic Structure and the Periodic Table

Q2 a) Dead plant material.
b) The CO_2 released when biogas is burnt is balanced out by the CO_2 removed from the atmosphere when the plants photosynthesised.
Q3 a)

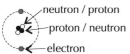

b) Alkanes have no double C=C bond but alkenes do.
Q4 a) cracking
b) E.g. decane → propene + heptane
$C_{10}H_{22} \rightarrow C_3H_6 + C_7H_{16}$
Q5 a) Lots of small molecules (monomers) join up to make long chain molecules (polymers).
b) Name: poly(chloroethene)

--C-C-C-C-C-C-C-C--

c) E.g. it's difficult to get rid of them. / They fill up landfill sites.
Q6 a) i) acidic
ii) alkaline
b) Milk of magnesia is alkaline, so it can neutralise the excess acid that causes indigestion.
Q7 a) i) magnesium chloride
ii) neutralisation
b) sulfuric acid / H_2SO_4
c) Metal oxides and metal hydroxides are usually **bases**.
Q8 a) calcium carbonate + hydrochloric acid → calcium chloride + water + carbon dioxide
b) By bubbling the gas produced through a delivery tube into limewater. The limewater would turn cloudy to show the presence of CO_2.

C2a Topic 1 — Atomic Structure and the Periodic Table

Page 51 — Atoms

Q1
neutron / proton
proton / neutron
electron

Q2

Particle	Mass	Charge
Proton	1	+1
Neutron	1	0
Electron	$\frac{1}{2000}$	−1

Q3 a) zero / 0
b) protons, electrons
c) tiny
Q4 a) nucleus
b) electron
c) electron
d) neutron

Pages 52-53 — Electron Shells

Q1 a) i) True
ii) False
iii) True
iv) False
v) False

b) ii) The lowest energy levels are always filled first.
iv) Atoms are more likely to react when they have partially filled shells.
v) A maximum of two electrons can occupy the first shell.
Q2 The innermost electron shell should be filled first. / There should be two electrons in the inner shell. The outer shell contains too many electrons. / The outer shell can hold a maximum of 8 electrons.
Q3

Element	Electronic configuration
Beryllium	2.2
Oxygen	2.6
Silicon	2.8.4
Boron	2.3
Aluminium	2.8.3
Argon	2.8.8

Q4 a) 2.8.7
b)

c) It doesn't have a full outer shell.
Q5
a) b) c)
d) e) f)
g) h) i)

Page 54 — Elements

Q1 atom, protons, atomic, mass
Q2 copper and oxygen
Q3 You would subtract the atomic number (the number of protons) from the mass number (the number of protons and neutrons).
Q4

Element	Symbol	Mass Number	Number of Protons	Number of Electrons	Number of Neutrons
Sodium	Na	23	11	11	12
Oxygen	O	16	8	8	8
Neon	Ne	20	10	10	10
Calcium	Ca	40	20	20	20

Page 55 — Isotopes and Relative Atomic Mass

Q1 isotopes, element, protons, neutrons
Q2 W and Y. These two atoms have the same number of protons (6) but different numbers of neutrons.
Q3 Relative atomic mass means — the average mass of the atoms of that element including the isotopes. Relative abundance means — how much there is of each isotope compared to the total amount of the element in the world.
Q4 $(35 \times 3) + (37 \times 1) = 142$
$142 \div 4 = \mathbf{35.5}$

C2a Topic 2 — Ionic Compounds and Analysis

Page 56 — A Brief History of the Periodic Table

Q1 table, properties
Q2 a) i) True
ii) False
b) Elements with similar properties appeared in the same vertical groups.
Q3 a) He wanted to place elements with similar properties in the same vertical groups. To make this work, he had to leave gaps.
b) germanium, 5.32 g/cm^3

Page 57 — The Periodic Table

Q1 a) horizontal
b) metals
c) right
d) similar
Q2 a) True
b) False
c) False
d) False
Q3 Any two from: helium, neon, krypton, xenon, radon.
Q4 a) Any one from: sodium, magnesium, aluminium, phosphorus, sulphur, chlorine, argon.
b) Any one from: lithium, sodium, rubidium, caesium, francium.
c) Any one from: beryllium, magnesium, calcium, strontium, barium, radium.
Q5 a) 7
b) The group number is always equal to the number of electrons in the outer shell.

C2a Topic 2 — Ionic Compounds and Analysis

Pages 58-59 — Ionic Bonding

Q1 elements, compounds, ionic, anions/cations, cations/anions
Q2 An ion is a positively or negatively charged atom or group of atoms.
Q3 a) False
b) True
c) True
d) False
e) True
Q4 a) Group 1
b) one
c) 1+
Q5 a) two
b) two
c)

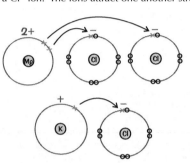

Q6 a) i) one
ii) two
iii) one
b) i) two
ii) one
iii) one

Q7 a) two
b) losing
c) 2^+
d) cation
e) can't
f) can

Pages 60-61 — Ionic Compounds

Q1

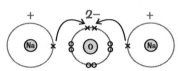

Q2 The sodium gives away its outer electron becoming an Na^+ ion. The chlorine atom picks up the electron, becoming a Cl^- ion. The ions attract one another strongly.

Q3

Q4 a) A regular lattice arrangement.
b) strong, positive, negative, large
Q5 a)

	Conducts electricity?
When solid	No
When dissolved in water	Yes
When molten	Yes

b) Magnesium oxide is an ionic compound. When it is molten or in solution, the ions separate and are free to move about, so they'll carry electric current. When it is solid the ions are held rigidly so they aren't free to move and conduct electricity.
Q6 Calcium chloride, because the ions in ionic compounds are held together by strong bonds/strong electrostatic forces. It takes a lot of energy to break these bonds so they have high melting points.

Page 62 — Naming Compounds and Finding Formulas

Q1 a) two, -IDE, oxygen, -ATE
b) i) potassium, nitrogen, oxygen
ii) calcium, carbon, oxygen
Q2 BeS, K_2S, BeI_2, KI
Q3 a) KBr
b) $FeCl_2$
c) CaF_2
d) Na_2CO_3
e) $Fe_2(SO_4)_3$
Q4 1−

C2a Topic 3 — Covalent Compounds and Separation Techniques

Page 63 — Preparing Insoluble Salts

Q1   C

Q2 a)   **silver nitrate** + **sodium chloride** → silver chloride + **sodium nitrate**

b)   The silver chloride must be filtered out of the solution. It needs to be washed and then dried on filter paper.

Q3 a)

Salt	Soluble	Salt	Soluble
copper nitrate	✓	calcium chloride	✓
lead nitrate	✓	calcium nitrate	✓
sodium carbonate	✓	lead sulfate	✗
copper carbonate	✗	sodium sulfate	✓

b) i)   lead sulfate, sodium nitrate

ii)   You would see a precipitate form. This is because lead nitrate, sodium sulfate and sodium nitrate are soluble but lead sulfate is insoluble so it will precipitate out.

Page 64 — Barium Meal and Flame Tests

Q1   toxic, insoluble, bloodstream, opaque, gut, blockages, meal

Q2 a)   Clean the wire loop using hydrochloric acid. If the substance is a solid, you may moisten the wire using hydrochloric acid to help the solid stick. Dip the wire loop in the sample and put it into the clear blue part of a Bunsen flame and observe.

b)   There could be other substances on the wire that might produce a different flame colour to the test substance.

Q3 a)   brick-red flame — Ca^{2+}
yellow/orange flame — Na^+
blue-green flame — Cu^{2+}
lilac flame — K^+

b)   potassium nitrate

Page 65 — Testing for Negative Ions and Spectroscopy

Q1   acid, carbon dioxide, limewater

Q2 a)   dilute hydrochloric acid, barium chloride

b)   a white precipitate (of barium sulfate)

Q3   By adding dilute nitric acid to a solution of the compound, and then adding some silver nitrate solution. If the compound contains chloride ions a white precipitate will form.

Q4 a) $Ag^+_{(aq)} + Cl^-_{(aq)} \rightarrow AgCl_{(s)}$

b) $2HCl_{(aq)} + Na_2CO_{3(s)} \rightarrow 2NaCl_{(aq)} + H_2O_{(l)} + CO_{2(g)}$

c) $Ba^{2+}_{(aq)} + SO_4^{2-}_{(aq)} \rightarrow BaSO_{4(s)}$

Q5 a)   E.g. rubidium, caesium

b)   E.g. it can detect very small amounts of elements.

C2a Topic 3 — Covalent Compounds and Separation Techniques

Page 66 — Covalent Bonding

Q1 a)   true
b)   true
c)   true
d)   false
e)   true

Q2

Atom	Carbon	Chlorine	Hydrogen	Nitrogen	Oxygen
Number of electrons needed to fill outer shell	4	1	1	3	2

Q3 a)

b)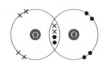

c)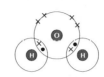

d)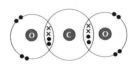

e)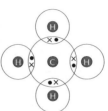

Q4   Sharing electrons allows both atoms to achieve the stable 'full outer shell' of electrons.

Page 67 — Covalent Substances — Two Kinds

Q1   small, strong, weak, easy

Q2 a)   low — the inter-molecular forces are weak and so the molecules can be easily parted from each other.

b)   don't conduct — there are no ions.

Q3   uncharged atoms, strong, high, insoluble

Q4 a)   As only three out of each of carbon's four outer electrons are used in bonds, there are lots of spare electrons. This makes graphite a good conductor of electricity.

b)   Each carbon atom forms four covalent bonds in a very rigid giant covalent structure, which makes diamond very hard.

c)   In graphite, sheets of carbon atoms are free to slide over each other. However, in diamond the carbon atoms are held rigidly and can't slide over each other.

Page 68 — Classifying Elements and Compounds

Q1

Property	Ionic Lattice	Giant Molecular	Simple Molecular
High melting and boiling points	✓	✓	✗
Can conduct electricity when solid	✗	✗ except graphite	✗
Can conduct electricity when molten	✓	✗ except graphite	✗

Q2 a) i)   A / B / F.

ii)   It has a low melting and boiling point because of weak intermolecular forces. It doesn't conduct electricity because it doesn't consist of ions or have free electrons.

b) i)   C

ii)   It has a very high melting point and boiling point. This is due to the strong covalent bonds in a giant molecular structure. Also, it doesn't conduct electricity when solid or liquid because there are no free electrons.

C2b Topic 4 — Groups in the Periodic Table

Page 69 — Separation Techniques

Q1 a) Doesn't separate out into layers when allowed to stand — Miscible — Fractional distillation
Separates out into layers when allowed to stand — Immiscible — Separating funnel
b) B
Q2 a) 1. Air is filtered to remove dust.
2. Air is cooled to -200 °C.
3. Carbon dioxide freezes and is removed. Water vapour condenses and is removed.
4. Liquefied air enters the fractionating column and is heated slowly.
b) mixture, boiling points
c) E.g. oxygen, nitrogen.

Page 70 — Chromatography

Q1 a) Put spots of the inks to be tested on a pencil baseline on filter paper. Put the paper in a beaker containing a solvent. The baseline must be kept above the level of the solvent.
b) solvent, spots, chromatogram
c) suspects 1 and 3
Q2 a) $31 \div 70 = \mathbf{0.44}$
b) $54 \div 70 = \mathbf{0.77}$

Pages 71-72 — Mixed Questions — C2a Topics 1, 2 & 3

Q1 a) 1
b) Group 2
c) Group 7
d)

Period	Group 1	Group 2	Group 3	Group 7	Group 0
2	Li 2.1	Be 2.2	B 2.3	F 2.7	Ne 2.8
3	Na 2.8.1	Mg 2.8.2	Al 2.8.3	Cl 2.8.7	Ar 2.8.8

Q2 a) Isotopes are different atomic forms of the same element, which have the same number of protons but different numbers of neutrons.
b) They are averages of the atomic masses of the different isotopes of that element, so it doesn't always work out as a whole number.
c)

isotope	number of protons	number of neutrons	number of electrons
^{1}H	1	0	1
^{2}H	1	1	1
^{3}H	1	2	1

d) i) The atomic number is the number of protons that the atom contains.
ii) All isotopes of an element have the same number of protons and therefore the same atomic number.
Q3 a) He would see a brick-red flame.
b) That the compound contains Cu^{2+} ions.
c) He could add dilute hydrochloric acid/HCl to the compound, followed by barium chloride/$BaCl_2$ and look for a white precipitate.
d) i) $Ba^{2+}_{(aq)} + SO_4^{2-}_{(aq)} \rightarrow BaSO_{4(s)}$
ii) $CuSO_4$
Q4 a)

b) i) LiF
ii) ionic bonding

C2b Topic 4 — Groups in the Periodic Table

Page 73 — Properties of Metals

Q1 a) the transition metals
b) They conduct electricity well.
c) E.g. they are colourful.
Q2 a)

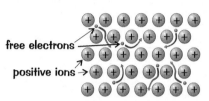

free electrons
positive ions

b) The electrons are delocalised so are able to move freely.
Q3 Any three from: good conductor of electricity / easily bendable / malleable / high melting point.

Pages 74-75 — Group 1 — The Alkali Metals

Q1 a)

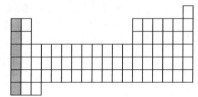

b) E.g. they're soft, they have low melting points compared with other metals.
c) (least) lithium, sodium, potassium (most).
d) As you go down Group 1, the lone electron is in a shell that is further from the nucleus. As they're further apart the attraction between the positively charged nucleus and the negatively charged electron decreases. The electron is easier to get rid of, making the element more reactive.
Q2 a) i) Metal B is the most reactive, because it takes the least time to react completely with the water and disappear.
ii) A = sodium, B = potassium, C = lithium.
b) i) sodium hydroxide, hydrogen
ii) The statement is not correct. Rubidium is further down Group 1 than metal B (potassium), so it is more reactive and will take less time to react with water.
Q3 one, potassium, hydroxide, hydrogen
Q4 a) lithium + water → lithium hydroxide + hydrogen
b) $2Li + 2H_2O \rightarrow 2LiOH + H_2$
c) alkaline
Q5 a) i) francium
ii) It's further down Group 1 and the alkali metals increase in reactivity as you go down the group.
b) Both metals are highly reactive with water. The oil will stop them coming into contact with water.

Pages 76-77 — Group 7 — The Halogens

Q1

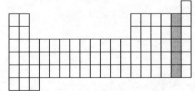

Q2 Bromine — orange liquid — quite reactive
Chlorine — green gas — very reactive
Iodine — grey solid — least reactive

C2b Topic 5 — Chemical Reactions

Q3 a) false
  b) true
  c) true
  d) false
  e) false
Q4 a) hydrogen chloride
  b) acidic
Q5 a) metal halides
  b) i) aluminium
   ii) iodine
   iii) magnesium fluoride
  c) i) $2Al + 3Br_2 \rightarrow 2AlBr_3$
   ii) $2K + I_2 \rightarrow 2KI$
   iii) $Mg + F_2 \rightarrow MgF_2$
Q6 a) Chlorine is a more reactive element than bromine, so the bromine can't displace it from the potassium chloride and there is no reaction.
  b) Bromine is a more reactive element than iodine. The more reactive bromine displaces the less reactive iodine from the compound to give potassium bromide, leaving the iodine in solution.
  c) $Br_2 + 2KI \rightarrow I_2 + 2KBr$

Page 78 — Group 0 — The Noble Gases

Q1 The far-right column of the periodic table.
Q2

Element	Boiling point (°C)	Density (g/cm³)
Helium	-269	0.0002
Neon	-246	0.0009
Argon	-186	0.0018

Q3 a) E.g. the noble gases are colourless, are non-flammable and don't easily react with anything, so they're very difficult to detect.
  b) chemical reactions, air, air, gases, fractional distillation
  c) Elements generally react in order to lose or gain enough electrons to give them a full outer shell. Noble gases already have a full outer shell of electrons so they do not need to react with anything.

C2b Topic 5 — Chemical Reactions

Pages 79-80 — Energy Transfer in Reactions

Q1 a) give out, heat, rise, temperature
  b) i) endothermic
   ii) exothermic
   iii) exothermic
   iv) endothermic
Q2 take in, heat, fall/decrease, temperature
Q3 Bond breaking — endothermic — heat energy must be supplied to break the bonds. Bond forming — exothermic — heat energy is released when new bonds are formed.
Q4 a) exothermic
  b) A–C, because more heat energy is released when this bond forms than is taken in when the A–B bond is broken.
Q5 a) Energy is taken in.
  b) Energy is given out.
  c) Burning methane is an exothermic process (this is true of all fuels) — when methane burns it gives out heat.
  d) B
Q6 a) X
  b) N
  c) X
  d) N

Page 81 — Energy Changes and Measuring Temperature

Q1 a) A, C and D
  b) B and E
  c) D
  d) B
Q2 a) i) To ensure that they are the same temperature before beginning the reaction.
   ii) The cotton wool insulates the cup and the lid is used to reduce the energy lost by evaporation.
   iii) Some energy is always lost or gained from the surroundings.
  b) i) temperature change = maximum temperature – start temperature = 31 °C – 21 °C = **10 °C**
   ii) neutralisation, exothermic

Page 82 — Rates of Reaction

Q1 a) higher
  b) lower
  c) decreases
  d) does
Q2 a) i) Z
   ii) The gas produced by the reaction was given off more quickly, shown by the steeper curve. / The reaction finished more quickly, shown by the curve levelling off sooner.
  b) Because the same mass of marble (and the same amount of acid) reacted each time.
  c) The curve should have the same initial slope as curve Z, but show that a larger volume of gas is produced, e.g. like this:

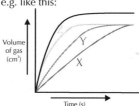

Q3 a) More reactants were used and so more products (including the gas) were formed.
  b) Reaction Q might have been carried out at a higher temperature / one of the reactants may have been more concentrated / a catalyst might have been used / a solid reactant might have had a smaller surface area.

Pages 83-84 — Rates of Reaction Experiments

Q1 increase, faster, surface area, react.
Q2 a) B
  b) Curve should be between curves A and B. It should level off at same height.
  c) $CaCO_3 + 2HCl \rightarrow CaCl_2 + CO_2 + H_2O$
  d) No, you cannot tell if it was a fair test. The same mass of marble chips was used each time but it is not known if the same concentration of HCl was used each time or if the temperature was kept constant.
  e) The volume of gas produced will increase.

C2b Topic 6 — Quantitative Chemistry

Q3 a) To improve the reliability of his results.
b) i)

Time (s)	Experiment 1 — loss in mass (g)	Experiment 2 — loss in mass (g)	Average loss in mass (g)
5	1.1	0.9	1.0
10	1.6	1.8	1.7
15	2.7	2.3	2.5
20	3.4	2.8	3.1
25	3.6	3.4	3.5
30	3.6	3.4	3.5

ii)

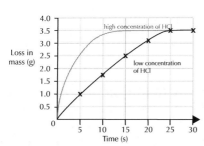

c) C

Page 85 — Rates of Reaction Experiments and Catalysts

Q1 a) faster
b) 145 s
Q2 a) A catalyst is a substance which changes the speed of a reaction, without being used up in the reaction.
b) i) R
ii) Reaction R has the steepest graph, so it is the fastest reaction and so must have used the most effective catalyst.
Q3 a) Catalytic converters increase the rate at which carbon monoxide and unburnt fuel in vehicle exhaust gases react with oxygen in the air to produce carbon dioxide and water.
b) E.g. they have a large surface area, they work best at high temperatures.

Page 86 — Collision Theory

Q1 a) collide
b) energy
c) faster, more
d) rate
Q2 increasing the temperature — makes the particles move faster so they collide more often.
decreasing the concentration — means fewer particles of reactant are present, so fewer collisions occur.
adding a catalyst — provides a surface for particles to stick to and lowers the energy required by the particles to react.
increasing the surface area — gives particles a bigger area of solid reactant to react with.
Q3 a) i) increase
ii) Increasing the pressure makes the particles more squashed up together, so there is more chance of them colliding and reacting.
b) E.g.

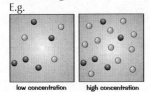

low concentration   high concentration

Q4 a) false
b) true
c) false
d) true

C2b Topic 6 — Quantitative Chemistry

Page 87 — Relative Formula Mass

Q1 a) 24
b) 20
c) 16
d) 1
e) 12
f) 63.5
g) 39
h) 40
i) 35.5
Q2 Element A is helium.
Element B is $(3 \times 4) = 12$ = carbon.
Element C is $(4 \times 4) = 16$ = oxygen.
Q3 a) You add the relative atomic masses of all the atoms in the compound together.
b) i) $(2 \times 1) + 16 = \mathbf{18}$
ii) $40 + (35.5 \times 2) = \mathbf{111}$
iii) $39 + 16 + 1 = \mathbf{56}$
iv) $1 + 14 + (3 \times 16) = \mathbf{63}$
v) $(2 \times 1) + 32 + (4 \times 16) = \mathbf{98}$
vi) $14 + (4 \times 1) + 14 + (3 \times 16) = \mathbf{80}$
vii) $(27 \times 2) + (32 \times 3) + (16 \times 4 \times 3) = \mathbf{342}$
Q4 $2XOH + H_2 = 114$
$2 \times (X + 16 + 1) + (2 \times 1) = 114$
$2 \times (X + 17) + 2 = 114$
$2 \times (X + 17) = 112$
$X + 17 = 56$
$X = 39$
so, X = **potassium**

Page 88 — Two Formula Mass Calculations

Q1 a) Percentage mass of an element in a compound =
$$\frac{A_r \times \text{No. of atoms (of that element)} \times 100}{M_r \text{ (of whole compound)}}$$
b) i) $(14 \times 2) \div [14 + (4 \times 1) + 14 + (3 \times 16)] \times 100 = 35\%$
ii) $(4 \times 1) \div [14 + (4 \times 1) + 14 + (3 \times 16)] \times 100 = 5\%$
iii) $(3 \times 16) \div [14 + (4 \times 1) + 14 + (3 \times 16)] \times 100 = 60\%$
Q2 a) $14 \div (14 + 16) \times 100 = 47\%$
b)

	Nitrogen	Oxygen
Mass (g)	30.4	69.6
$\div A_r$	$(30.4 \div 14) = 2.17$	$(69.6 \div 16) = 4.35$
Ratio	1	2

empirical formula = NO_2

Q3

	Aluminium	Bromine
Mass (g)	31.9	288.1
$\div A_r$	$(31.9 \div 27) = 1.2$	$(288.1 \div 80) = 3.6$
Ratio	1	3

empirical formula = $AlBr_3$

Q4 a) $A = (3 \times 16) \div [(2 \times 56) + (3 \times 16)] \times 100 = 30\%$
$B = 16 \div [(2 \times 1) + 16)] \times 100 = 88\%$
$C = (3 \times 16) \div [40 + 12 + (3 \times 16)] \times 100 = 48\%$
b) B

C2b Topic 6 — Quantitative Chemistry

Pages 89-90 — Calculating Masses in Reactions

Q1 a) $2Mg + O_2 \rightarrow 2MgO$
b)

$2Mg$	$2MgO$
$2 \times 24 = 48$	$2 \times (24 + 16) = 80$
$48 \div 48 = 1g$	$80 \div 48 = 1.67\ g$
$1 \times 10 = 10\ g$	$1.67 \times 10 = \textbf{16.7 g}$

Q2

$4Na$	$2Na_2O$
$4 \times 23 = 92$	$2 \times [(2 \times 23) + 16] = 124$
$92 \div 124 = 0.74\ g$	$124 \div 124 = 1\ g$
$0.74 \times 2 = \textbf{1.48 g}$	$1 \times 2 = 2\ g$

Q3 a) $2Al + Fe_2O_3 \rightarrow Al_2O_3 + 2Fe$
b)

Fe_2O_3	$2Fe$
$[(2 \times 56) + (3 \times 16)] = 160$	$2 \times 56 = 112$
$160 \div 160 = 1\ g$	$112 \div 160 = 0.7$
$1 \times 20 = 20\ g$	$0.7 \times 20 = \textbf{14 g}$

Q4 $CaCO_3 \rightarrow CaO + CO_2$

$CaCO_3$	CaO
$40 + 12 + (3 \times 16) = 100$	$40 + 16 = 56$
$100 \div 56 = 1.786\ kg$	$56 \div 56 = 1\ kg$
$1.786 \times 100 = \textbf{178.6 kg}$	$1 \times 100 = 100\ kg$

Q5 a)

C	$2CO$
12	$2 \times (12 + 16) = 56$
$12 \div 12 = 1\ g$	$56 \div 12 = 4.67\ g$
$1 \times 10 = 10\ g$	$4.67 \times 10 = 46.7\ g$

$46.7\ g$ of CO is produced in stage B — all this is used in stage C.

$3CO$	$3CO_2$
$3 \times (12 + 16) = 84$	$3 \times [12 + (16 \times 2)] = 132$
$84 \div 84 = 1$	$132 \div 84 = 1.57$
$1 \times 46.7 = 46.7$	$1.57 \times 46.7 = \textbf{73.4 g}$

b) It could be recycled and used in stage B.
Q6 a) $2NaOH + H_2SO_4 \rightarrow Na_2SO_4 + 2H_2O$
b)

$2NaOH$	Na_2SO_4
$2 \times (23 + 16 + 1) = 80$	$(2 \times 23) + 32 + (4 \times 16) = 142$
$80 \div 142 = 0.56\ g$	$142 \div 142 = 1\ g$
$0.56 \times 75 = \textbf{42.3 g}$	$1 \times 75 = 75\ g$

c)

H_2SO_4	$2H_2O$
$(2 \times 1) + 32 + (4 \times 16) = 98$	$2 \times [(2 \times 1) + 16] = 36$
$98 \div 98 = 1\ g$	$36 \div 98 = 0.367\ g$
$1 \times 50 = 50\ g$	$0.367 \times 50 = \textbf{18.4 g}$

Pages 91-92 — Percentage Yield

Q1 a) The yield of a reaction is the mass of product it produces.
b) i) Percentage yield = (actual yield ÷ theoretical yield) × 100.
ii) $(1.2 \div 2.7) \times 100 = \textbf{44.4\%}$
Q2 a) $(6 \div 15) \times 100 = \textbf{40\%}$
b) Any two from: e.g. there may have been losses during preparation when a small amount of the original reactants may have been left behind in their original containers when they were transferred to another / when the solid was filtered out, some of it will have been left on the original piece of filter paper / there may have been unwanted reactions due to impurities / carrying out the reaction under different conditions may change the products made / the reaction may have been incomplete so not all of the reactants were converted to products.
Q3 a) A = $(3.00 \div 3.33) \times 100 = \textbf{90.1\%}$
B = $(3.18 \div 3.33) \times 100 = \textbf{95.5\%}$
C = $(3.05 \div 3.33) \times 100 = \textbf{91.6\%}$
D = $(3.15 \div 3.33) \times 100 = \textbf{94.6\%}$
b) A, C
Q4 a) $(3.4 \div 4.0) \times 100 = \textbf{85\%}$
b) $(6.4 \div 7.2) \times 100 = \textbf{88.9\%}$
c) $3.6 \div c = 0.8.$ So $3.6 = 0.8 \times c$
So $c = 3.6 \div 0.8 = \textbf{4.5}$
d) $d \div 6.5 = 0.9.$ So $d = 0.9 \times 6.5 = \textbf{5.85}$

Q5 waste, harmful, environment, expensive, yield, commercially, speed
Q6 a) $CaCO_3 \rightarrow CaO + CO_2$
b)

$CaCO_3$	CaO
$40 + 12 + (16 \times 3) = 100$	$40 + 16 = 56$
$100 \div 100 = 1$ tonne	$56 \div 100 = 0.56$ tonnes
$1 \times 100 = 100$ tonnes	$0.56 \times 100 = \textbf{56 tonnes}$

c) $(42 \div 56) \times 100 = \textbf{75\%}$
d) E.g. limestone is not a pure substance, so there will be other reactions happening and other products being formed.

Pages 93-94 — Mixed Questions — C2b Topics 4, 5 & 6

Q1 a) E.g. a gas syringe could be used to measure the volume of CO_2 gas given off by the reaction.
b) A
c) The reaction slows and stops, as all the reactants are used up.
d) i) Curve above for the higher temperature.
Curve below for the lower temperature.
All should end at the same point for end of reaction.
For example:

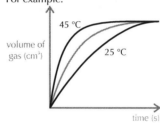

ii) When the temperature increases the particles all move quicker. The particles will have more frequent collisions and the rate of reaction will increase.
e) E.g. concentration of a solution, presence of a catalyst, surface area of a solid reactant
Q2 a) One bond between the two iodine atoms and one bond between the two hydrogen atoms.
b) Two new bonds between a hydrogen atom and an iodine atom.
c) Breaking bonds is endothermic.
d) It will fall because endothermic reactions take in energy from their surroundings in the form of heat.
Q3 a) A catalyst works by lowering the energy required by the reactants to react. This makes it easier for the reaction to happen and increases the rate of reaction.
b) A powder would be better because there is a larger surface area for the reacting particles to stick to where they can collide.
Q4 a)

	Silicon	Chlorine
Mass (g)	1.4	7.1
÷ A_r	$(1.4 \div 28) = 0.05$	$(7.1 \div 35.5) = 0.2$
Ratio	1	4

Empirical formula = $\textbf{SiCl}_4$
b) $(35.5 \times 4) \div [(35.5 \times 4) + 28] \times 100 = \textbf{83.5\%}$
c) $Si + 2Cl_2 \rightarrow SiCl_4$
d) $6.5 \div 8.5 \times 100 = \textbf{76\%}$
Q5 a) $Cl_2 + 2KBr \rightarrow Br_2 + 2KCl$
b) The green solution would turn orange.
c) Bromine is less reactive than chlorine, so it doesn't displace it from the solution.

C3a Topic 1 — Qualitative Analysis

C3a Topic 1 — Qualitative Analysis

Page 95 — Analysing Substances

Q1   qualitative, only, sample, much, quantitative
Q2   Any two from: e.g. blood tests are carried out to diagnose disease / blood tests are carried out to monitor a patient's general health / blood tests are carried out by the police to check the alcohol content of the blood / water companies analyse tap water for dangerous chemicals.
Q3 a)   So that the result you get could only be for one possible ion.
  b) i)   qualitative
     ii)   qualitative
  c)   aluminium sulfate

Pages 96-97 — Testing for Ions

Q1 a)   a white precipitate
  b) $CaCl_2$ (aq) + 2NaOH (aq) → $Ca(OH)_2$ (s) + 2NaCl (aq)
  c) Ca^{2+} (aq) + 2OH⁻ (aq) → $Ca(OH)_2$ (s)
Q2 a)

Metal Cation	Colour of Precipitate
Fe^{2+}	green
Cu^{2+}	blue
Fe^{3+}	brown
Al^{3+}	white

  b) Fe^{2+} (aq) + 2OH⁻ (aq) → $Fe(OH)_2$ (s)
  c) Fe^{3+} (aq) + 3OH⁻ (aq) → $Fe(OH)_3$ (s)
  d)   Cilla would see a white precipitate at first, but it would redissolve in excess NaOH to form a colourless solution.
Q3   By adding dilute nitric acid to a solution of the compound, and then adding some silver nitrate solution. If the compound contains Cl⁻ ions a white precipitate will form. If it contains Br⁻ ions a cream precipitate will form. If it contains I⁻ ions a yellow precipitate will form.
Q4 a) $CuSO_4$
  b) $Al_2(SO_4)_3$
  c) $FeSO_4$
  d) $FeCl_3$
  e) NH_4Cl
  f) $CaCl_2$
Q5 a)   E.g. dissolve a small quantity of the solid in water. Add a few drops of sodium hydroxide solution. Warm the resulting mixture, testing any gas given off with a damp piece of universal indicator paper.
  b)   The solid dissolves to produce a colourless solution. A white precipitate of calcium hydroxide is produced when the sodium hydroxide solution is added. A pungent smelling gas (ammonia) is given off when the mixture is warmed. This gas turns the damp universal indicator paper purple.
  c) Ca^{2+} (aq) + 2OH⁻ (aq) → $Ca(OH)_2$ (s)
     NH_4^+ (aq) + OH⁻ (aq) → NH_3 (g) + H_2O (l)

C3a Topic 2 — Quantitative Analysis

Page 98 — Measuring Amounts

Q1 a)   mass, relative formula mass
  b)   mass in g = number of moles × M_r
  c) i)   **63.5 g**
     ii)   3 × (2 × 35.5) = **213 g**
     iii)   2 × [1 + 14 + (16 × 3)] = **126 g**
     iv)   2.5 × (23 + 16 + 1) = **100 g**
     v)   0.5 × [40 + 12 + (16 × 3)] = **50 g**
Q2 a)   number of moles = $\dfrac{\text{mass in g}}{M_r}$
  b) i)   20 ÷ 40 = **0.5 moles**
     ii)   112 ÷ 32 = **3.5 moles**
     iii)   200 ÷ (63.5 + 16) = **2.52 moles**
     iv)   110 ÷ [12 + (2 × 16)] = **2.5 moles**
  c) i)   2 × 23 = **46 g**
     ii)   1.25 × 27 = **33.75 g**
     iii)   0.75 × (24 + 16) = **30 g**
     iv)   0.025 × [207 + (35.5 × 2)] = **6.95 g**

Page 99 — Solutions and Concentrations

Q1 a)   2 ÷ 4 = **0.5 g/dm³**
  b)   4.6 ÷ 2 = **2.3 g/dm³**
  c)   0.8 ÷ (500 / 1000) = **1.6 g/dm³**
  d)   0.2 ÷ (100 / 1000) = **2.0 g/dm³**
Q2 a) i) M_r of NaOH = 23 + 16 + 1 = 40
     2 × 40 = **80 g/dm³**
     ii) M_r of $C_6H_{12}O_6$ = (6 × 12) + 12 + (6 × 16) = 180
     0.1 × 180 = **18 g/dm³**
  b) M_r of HCl = 1 + 35.5 = 36.5
     3.8 ÷ 36.5 = **0.104 mol/dm³**
Q3 a)   She would weigh the basin and contents and then reheat and reweigh until there is no further change in mass. This shows that all the water has evaporated.
  b)   By subtracting the mass of the pre-weighed basin from the final mass of the basin and contents.

Page 100 — Hard Water

Q1 a)   false
  b)   false
  c)   false
  d)   true
Q2 a) Ca^{2+}, Mg^{2+}
  b)   An ion exchange resin has lots of sodium ions or hydrogen ions which are exchanged for calcium ions and magnesium ions, removing them from the water.
  c)   This works for both types of hardness.
Q3 a)   Tap water could contain metal ions which cause hardness. Distilled water is pure and contains no metal ions.
  b) i)   magnesium sulfate, calcium chloride
     ii)   These solutions formed a scum with soap solution. / More soap was needed to form a sustainable lather.

Page 101 — Titrations

Q1 a)   ...the flask is swirled regularly.
  b)   ...neutralisation reaction.
  c)   ...the concentration of an acid or base.
Q2   pipette filler, indicator, burette, neutralised, volume, acid
Q3 a)   H⁺ (aq) + OH⁻ (aq) → H_2O (l)
  b)   To make sure that the results were reliable.
  c)   Kolafizz

C3a Topic 3 — Electrolytic Processes

Page 102 — More on Titrations

Q1 a) $0.1 \times (20 \div 1000) = $ **0.002 moles**
b) $2HCl + Ca(OH)_2 \rightarrow CaCl_2 + 2H_2O$
c) 2, 1
d) $0.002 \div 2 = $ **0.001 moles**
e) $0.001 \div (50 \div 1000) = $ **0.02 mol/dm³**
f) Concentration $= 0.02 \times (40 + 32 + 2) = $ **1.48 g/dm³**
Q2 a) Moles KOH $= 0.1 \times (30 \div 1000) = 0.003$
Reaction equation: $H_2SO_4 + 2KOH \rightarrow K_2SO_4 + 2H_2O$
so $0.003 \div 2 = 0.0015$ moles of H_2SO_4.
concentration $= 0.0015 \div (10 \div 1000) = $ **0.15 mol/dm³**
b) Mass in grams $= 0.15 \times [2 + 32 + (16 \times 4)] = $ **14.7 g/dm³**

Page 103 — Preparing Soluble Salts

Q1 a) The solid no longer disappears and the excess solid will sink to the bottom of the flask.
b)

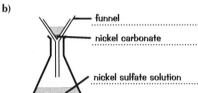

funnel
nickel carbonate
nickel sulfate solution

c) filtration
d) Heat the nickel sulfate solution gently to evaporate off the water.
e) i) As potassium hydroxide is a soluble salt, you can't tell when the reaction is finished — you can't just add an excess of solid to the acid and filter out what's left.
ii) You have to add exactly the right amount of alkali to just neutralise the acid so you must carry out a titration first to find out the exact amount of alkali needed. Then repeat using exactly the same volumes of alkali and acid so the salt isn't contaminated with indicator.

C3a Topic 3 — Electrolytic Processes

Page 104 — Electrolysis of Molten Substances

Q1 For electricity to flow through the electrolyte, the ions need to be free to move. In a solid, the ions are in fixed positions, whereas in a solution or molten they can move about.
Q2 a) i) True
ii) False
iii) True
iv) False
v) False
b) E.g. street lamps, coolant in some nuclear reactors.
Q3 a) i) bromide ion / Br^-
ii) $2Br^- \rightarrow Br_2 + 2e^-$
b) i) lead ion / Pb^{2+}
ii) $Pb^{2+} + 2e^- \rightarrow Pb$
Q4 a) e^-, Na — reduction
b) 2, Cu — reduction
c) 4, 2, 4 — oxidation

Page 105 — Electrolysis of Solutions

Q1 a) A: H^+
B: Cl^-
C: H_2
D: Cl_2
b) Cathode: $2H^+ + 2e^- \rightarrow H_2$
Anode: $2Cl^- \rightarrow Cl_2 + 2e^-$
Q2

Compound	Product formed at the:	
	cathode	anode
copper chloride solution	copper (s)	chlorine (g)
copper sulfate solution	copper (s)	oxygen (g)
sodium sulfate solution	hydrogen (g)	oxygen (g)

Q3 Molten compounds only contain one positive ion (a metal ion) which is discharged at the cathode and one negative ion which is discharged at the anode. The products of electrolysis always come from the compound. Aqueous solutions would also contain H^+ ions and OH^- ions from the water. So an aqueous solution can give products from these ions in water rather than the ions of the dissolved solid.

Page 106 — Electrolysis Using Copper Electrodes

Q1 The copper produced will have zinc impurities in it.
Q2 a) A — pure copper electrode
B — impure copper electrode
C — copper ions
D — copper sulfate solution
b) i) $Cu (s) \rightarrow Cu^{2+}(aq) + 2e^-$
ii) $Cu^{2+}(aq) + 2e^- \rightarrow Cu (s)$
c) The impurities are not charged (i.e. they are neutral) so they are not attracted to the cathode.
d) Electrode A is the anode. The mass of the anode decreases as copper ions are lost from it and move towards the cathode.

Page 107 — Electroplating

Q1 gold, appearance, corroding, unreactive
Q2 a) i) zinc
ii) copper
b) i) zinc sulfate
ii) Lily must use an electrolyte containing zinc ions as these will move towards the cathode and coat the copper rod.
Q3 a)

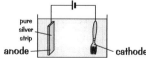

pure silver strip
anode
cathode

b) silver / Ag^+
c) i) $Ag \rightarrow Ag^+ + e^-$
ii) $Ag^+ + e^- \rightarrow Ag$

C3b Topic 4 — Gases, Reversible Reactions and Ammonia

Pages 108-110 — Mixed Questions — C3a Topics 1, 2 & 3

Q1 a) mass concentration (g/dm^3) = mass (g) / volume (dm^3)
= 0.1 / (238 ÷ 1000) = **0.42 g/dm³**

b) quantitative

Q2 a)

b) qualitative

c)

d) Al^{3+} (aq) + $3OH^-$ (aq) → $Al(OH)_3$ (s)
$Al(OH)_3$ (s) + OH^- (aq) → $Al(OH)_4^-$ (aq)

Q3 a) 24 + [2 × (14 + [16 × 3])] = **148**

b) i) Mg: 0.12 ÷ 24 = **0.005** moles
$Mg(NO_3)_2$: 0.74 ÷ 148 = **0.005** moles

ii) 0.025 × [1 + 14 + (16 × 3)] = **1.575 g**

Q4 a) B

b) A

c) Boiling removes temporary hardness from water. River A must contain sources of both permanent and temporary hardness. Once the temporary hardness was removed, less soap was needed to form a lasting lather.

d) i) permanent hardness

ii) By using an ion exchange resin.

Q5 a) electrolysis

b) The ions have to be free to move to carry the current. Ions cannot move in a solid since they are in fixed positions.

c) i) Electrode A: Pb^{2+} Electrode B: Br^-

ii) Pb^{2+} + $2e^-$ → Pb
$2Br^-$ → Br_2 + $2e^-$

Q6 a) X = pipette
Y = conical flask
Z = burette

b) i) Moles NaOH = 0.5 × (20 ÷ 1000) = 0.01 moles
NaOH + HCl → NaCl + H_2O, so there's also 0.01 moles of HCl. Concentration of HCl = 0.01 ÷ (25 ÷ 1000) = **0.4 mol/dm³**

ii) M_r HCl = 1 + 35.5 = 36.5
In 1 dm³: mass in grams = moles × M_r = 0.4 × 36.5 = **14.6 g/dm³**

C3b Topic 4 — Gases, Reversible Reactions and Ammonia

Page 111 — Calculating Volumes

Q1 a) 24 dm³

b) molar volume

c) i) 0.5 × 24 = **12 dm³**

ii) 6.25 × 24 = **150 dm³**

d) i) 0.24 ÷ 24 = **0.01 mol**

ii) 8 ÷ 24 = **0.33 mol**

Q2 a) moles of calcium hydroxide = mass ÷ M_r
= 0.37 ÷ 74 = 0.005 moles,
so moles of carbon dioxide needed = 0.005 moles
Mass of carbon dioxide = moles × M_r
= 0.005 × 44 = **0.22 g**

b) 1 mole of CO_2 occupies 24 dm³ at RTP, so 0.005 moles CO_2 occupies 24 × 0.005 = **0.12 dm³**

Q3 a) $S + O_2 → SO_2$

b) 32 + (2 × 16) = **64**

c)

	S	SO_2
M_r	32	64
÷ 32	1	2
× 144	144g	288g

So, volume of sulfur dioxide = (mass ÷ M_r) × 24
= (288 ÷ 64) × 24 = **108 dm³**

Pages 112-113 — Reversible Reactions

Q1 a) products, react, reactants

b) balance

c) closed, escape

Q2 a) true

b) false

c) true

d) false

Q3 a) i) A and B

ii) AB

b) i) Y

ii) X

c) A + B ⇌ AB

d) at the same rate

Q4 a) It takes in heat — all reversible reactions are exothermic in one direction and endothermic in the other.

b) left

c) Because one reaction is always exothermic and the other endothermic. A change in temperature will always favour one reaction more than the other.

d) It won't affect the position, as the volume (number of molecules) of products and reactants are the same.

Q5 a) i) Forward, because there are more molecules of reactants than of products in the forward direction.

ii) Increasing the pressure will give more SO_3, i.e. will shift the equilibrium in favour of the forward reaction.

b) B

c) It remains the same (because the speeds of the forward and the backward reactions increase equally).

Page 114 — The Haber Process

Q1 a) nitrogen, hydrogen

b) The left (reactants) side.

c) The pressure should be increased, as this will favour the reaction which produces less volume, i.e. the one which produces more ammonia.

Q2 a) It would be too expensive to build a plant strong enough to withstand the high pressure.

b) i) Raising the temperature will reduce the amount of ammonia formed.

ii) Because if a low temperature was used the reaction would be far too slow. This temperature gives an acceptable yield in an acceptable time.

Q3 a) nitrogenous fertilisers

b) E.g. fertiliser may stimulate the excessive growth of algae on the surface of the water. This layer of algae blocks the light so plants living below the surface may die as they can no longer photosynthesise. Decomposers feeding on the dead plants use up the oxygen in the water, causing fish to die.

C3b Topic 5 — Organic Chemistry

C3b Topic 5 — Organic Chemistry

Pages 115-116 — Homologous Series

Q1 general, elements, molecular, chemical, physical, boiling points

Q2 a)

methane CH_4

ethane C_2H_6

propane C_3H_8

H−C−C−C−H (with H above and below each C)

butane C_4H_{10}

H−C−C−C−C−H (with H above and below each C)

b) alkanes

Q3 a)

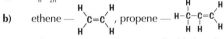

C_2H_5OH

b) $C_nH_{2n+1}OH$

Q4 a)

H−C with double bond O and OH

b) i) C_2H_5COOH
ii) CH_3COOH

Q5 a) C_nH_{2n}

b) ethene — C=C (with H's), propene — H−C−C=C (with H's)

c) Alkenes contain at least one double bond in their chain of carbon atoms.

Pages 117-118 — Production of Ethanol

Q1 a) i) carbohydrates
ii) enzyme
iii) temperature
iv) anaerobic
b) A

Q2 E.g. mix yeast and a solution of carbohydrate in a clean container. Seal the container to make sure no oxygen can reach the reaction mixture. Store the container in a warm place (between 30 °C and 40 °C). Eventually, the reaction will stop and the yeast will fall to the bottom of the container — collect the ethanol solution from the top.

Q3 a) fractional distillation
b) i) A — thermometer
B — fractionating column
ii) C — boiling / evaporation of the ethanol solution
D — cooling and condensation of ethanol vapour
c) E.g. the concentration of ethanol produced by fermentation is low, so fractional distillation is used to concentrate the ethanol.

Q4 a) E.g. fermentation uses a renewable resource (e.g. sugar beet or sugar cane) which will never run out.
b) E.g. the quality of the ethanol isn't great / it's expensive to concentrate and purify the ethanol produced.

Page 119 — Production and Issues of Ethanol

Q1 a) Ethene + steam → ethanol
b) E.g. ethanol is made continuously and quickly / high quality ethanol is produced / the ethanol needs little further processing / it's currently a cheap process.

Q2 Any three from: e.g. drink driving can cause death or serious injury / more police are needed to deal with drunken crowds / more doctors and nurses are needed to care for drunken patients / getting drunk can lead to irresponsible sexual behaviour / alcoholism can cause family breakdown and unemployment.

Q3 E.g. ethanol reduces the activity of the nervous system and can lead to unconsciousness and even coma. Alcohol can cause dehydration which damages brain cells and can cause a noticeable drop in brain function and long-term memory loss. Alcohol can also damage the liver leading to liver disease.

Page 120 — Ethene and Ethanoic Acid

Q1 a) $C_2H_5OH \rightarrow C_2H_4 + H_2O$
b) dehydration

Q2 a) The ethanol in wine that has been left open is oxidised to ethanoic acid, and vinegar is just dilute ethanoic acid.
b) E.g. flavouring/preserving foods.

Q3 a) i) ethanoic acid + calcium → calcium ethanoate + hydrogen
ii) $2CH_3COOH + Ca \rightarrow (CH_3COO)_2Ca + H_2$
b) $CH_3COOH + KOH \rightarrow CH_3COOK + H_2O$
c) sodium ethanoate, carbon dioxide, water
d) It will turn blue litmus paper red.

Page 121 — Esters

Q1 a) fleece
b) E.g. plastic bottles.

Q2 a) E.g. many esters have pleasant smells.
b) ethanol + ethanoic acid → ethyl ethanoate + water
c)

H−C−C (double bond O) O−C−C−H (with H's)

d) E.g. flavourings.

Page 122 — Uses of Esters

Q1 a) i) ester
ii) boiling, alkali
b) i) the hydrophilic head
ii) the hydrophobic tail
c) The hydrophobic tails dissolve into the oil but the hydrophilic heads stay on the outside of the oil and dissolve in the water. The soap molecules get the oil and water to mix.

Q2 a) Saturated oils have no C=C double bonds. Unsaturated oils have at least one.
b) i) catalytic hydrogenation
ii) E.g. the double bonds in liquid unsaturated oils are broken using high temperature and pressure with a catalyst and hydrogen is added to the molecules where the double bonds were. This produces more viscous saturated oils.
c) E.g. margarine

C3b Topic 5 — Organic Chemistry

Pages 123-124 — Mixed Questions — C3b Topics 4 & 5

Q1 a) glucose → ethanol + carbon dioxide

b) E.g. the product is of a high quality and does not need further processing / a more concentrated solution of ethanol can be produced.

c) Ethene is produced from crude oil, which is a non-renewable resource. Eventually it will begin to run out, and then the price of all the products made from it will increase dramatically.

Q2 a) One mole of any gas will always occupy 24 dm^3 at room temperature and atmospheric pressure.

b) i)

	O_2	H_2O_2
M_r	32	34
÷ 32	1	1.0626
× 3.8	3.8 g	4.04 g

volume of H_2O_2 = (mass / M_r) × 24 = (4.04 / 34) × 24 = **2.9 dm^3**

ii) 2.9 dm^3

c) 1 mole of H_2O_2 would occupy 24 dm^3.
So, 6.2 moles would occupy 6.2 × 24 = **148.8 dm^3**

Q3 a) i) ethanol + oxygen → ethanoic acid + water

ii) oxidation

b) $2CH_3COOH + Na_2CO_3 \rightarrow 2CH_3COONa + CO_2 + H_2O$

Q4 a) i) A group of compounds with the same general formula. They have similar chemical properties and show a gradual change in physical properties.

ii) They increase.

b) i) ethanoic acid + ethanol → ethyl ethanoate + water

ii)

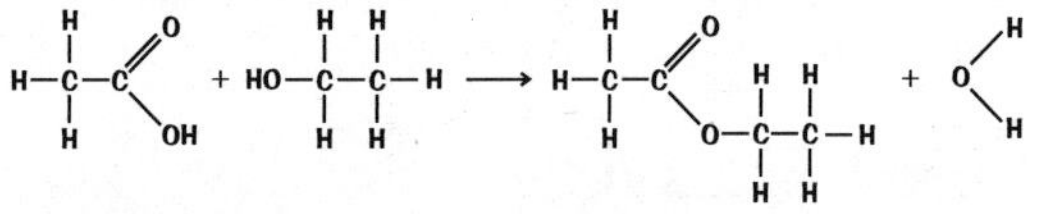

c) The ester is boiled with concentrated sodium hydroxide solution. They react to form a sodium salt of the long-chain carboxylic acid (soap) and water.

ISBN 978 1 84762 620 2

9 781847 626202

CEA44